TURN YOUR COMMON SENSE INTO BUSINESS SAVVY

JONATHAN JOSEPH JR.

The opinions expressed in this manuscript are solely the opinions of the author and do not represent the opinions or thoughts of the publisher. The author has represented and warranted full ownership and/or legal right to publish all the materials in this book.

Turn Your Common Sense Into Business Savvy
All Rights Reserved.
Copyright © 2014 Jonathan Joseph Jr.
v1.0

Cover Photo © 2014 thinkstockphotos.com. All rights reserved - used with permission.

This book may not be reproduced, transmitted, or stored in whole or in part by any means, including graphic, electronic, or mechanical without the express written consent of the publisher except in the case of brief quotations embodied in critical articles and reviews.

Outskirts Press, Inc.

http://www.outskirtspress.com

ISBN: 978-1-4787-3129-0

Outskirts Press and the "OP" logo are trademarks belonging to Outskirts Press, Inc.

PRINTED IN THE UNITED STATES OF AMERICA

CONTENTS

INTRODUCTION..1

1: IMAGE..2

2: THOUGHTS/IMAGINATION 6

3: COMMUNICATION..12

4: ATTITUDE/ENERGY..19

5: LOVE 24

INTRODUCTION

Why did you make the choice to read this book? Is it because you need help transforming your image? Do you feel like where you were raised effects your ability to be successful? What if I told you that how and where you were raised is to your advantage? There are 5 major principles that all successful people utilize in business and in life. It has taken me years to accumulate these 5 major principles and apply them to my life. Growing up I did not have anyone to show me these secrets. I now want to give back and help others gain the same level of success and personal growth. If you follow the 5 principles in this book you will enjoy success beyond your wildest dreams. In each chapter I will outline what you need to do in order to be the person you imagined. There is only one requirement. YOU MUST TAKE THE TIME AND EVALUATE HOW YOU FEEL AFTER EVERY CHAPTER! This is very important. As you read the book remember in order to be great you must first think and feel great.

1

IMAGE

Image is the first thing we look at as a society. Inside each of us is a need to be seen, heard, felt, and regarded physically. This desire is what makes you pay $200 dollars for a pair of Air Jordan's or $300 for a Coach bag. The major problem is most people can't afford these luxuries. So how can you improve your image if you can't afford the best quality products?

This chapter is not about your outside image, it's about your inside image. It's about the way you see yourself in your thoughts. If the mental vision of yourself could be shown on a TV monitor what would you be wearing? Would you have on a suit, sagging jeans, a dress, daisy dukes, or nothing at all? In order to change our outside image we must first change the mental image we have of ourselves. Too often we wear what the fashion experts tell us is hip or sexy. What we don't realize is that some of these styles are not work appropriate. This means in a perfect world we would have one style for the beach, one for casual events/going out, and one for business. Unfortunately, most of

IMAGE

us don't have money to have 3 different wardrobes. So what ends up happening? We wear what is considered to be casual wear in business settings because we are not aware of bargain shopping. Or we live outside of our financial means to wear designer clothing. This can lead to financial stress, or what I call commercial rage. Commercial rage is when you see a product you want advertised and you get angry because you can't afford it. Commercial rage is one of the contributing factors to most crimes in our inner cities.

Everyone has a right and the ability to have nice things. Just like a baby learns how to crawl before they can run. You must gradually move your mind into the freedom it seeks.

If you have $100 to spend on clothes a month buy something that you can use more than once. Why buy a shirt that you can only wear with jeans or shorts? Instead find a shirt that you can wear with jeans, shorts and dress pants. Get more "bang for your buck". In order to change your image you must first change the way you think. When you change the way you think and feel it brings success. Remember this; nothing in this universe is free. Your financial future doesn't require you to invest money to be successful; it requires you to change your thinking. If you make how you look a priority, no matter where you go people will notice and new doors will open.

I knew a man that was a director of operations for a 27 million dollar restaurant group. His name was

TURN YOUR COMMON SENSE
INTO BUSINESS SAVVY

Dave. Dave was the best dressed professional I ever met. When Dave decided to dress casual he was still the best dressed guy in the room. I knew I didn't have the body type to dress like Dave. I did however admire the impact that he had anytime he entered a room. I knew if I could dress like Dave I would impress the sophisticated ladies in the company. One day I got up the nerve to ask Dave where he did his shopping. I explained that I wanted to change my dress style to impress the ladies. Dave looked me square in the eyes and said "I don't dress for compliments or ladies I dress for money". I didn't know what to make of what he said. The next day I cornered Dave and asked him to explain what he meant by dressing for money. He said "In the work environment you have two choices when selecting a wardrobe". He continued.

"You can lose money buying top designer clothes that no one really notices or you can buy clothes realizing that the real designer name that matters is your own". What followed changed my life and set me on the yellow brick road of success. Dave told me that he shopped at three stores Wal-Mart, Target, and Marshalls. Here is what he did on a monthly basis. He took $50 out each paycheck for a total of $100 per month. He would add 2 outfits each month to his initial wardrobe. Buying different items from each store based on sales and his needs. He knew that his ties and socks were the items people noticed the most. He spent $35 on two dress pants, $40 on designer ties and socks

IMAGE

on sale, $25 on two dress shirts totaling $100. He then explained that most people buy expensive clothing because they think the fabric is better. Dave quickly dismissed that theory by saying "how you clean your clothes will determine the longevity". The shirts and pants should be washed but air dried. The fabric and stitching was not made to withstand the intense heat of the dryer. He said after one year you will have over 56 different outfit combinations. The last thing he said was "one thing you must remember people like attractive people, in other words sex sells". I wasn't sold on the whole sex sells thing at the time but, I did take his advice on dressing great for less. After one month of using this plan I got a promotion. I also got the attention of the lady co-workers and clients. It turned out to be the start of big things for me.

A former boss had this saying every time I would take a Friday night off from work. "You can lose a lot of time and money chasing beautiful women, but you will never lose beautiful women chasing money". I never forgot that saying but I apply it to my life in a different way. I look at my image as the money. If I keep my image the best, I will always have the audience I need to be successful. With success comes money and with money comes the amenities you seek. Don't fake it until you make it. Be yourself and know that your thoughts will achieve your goals. You don't have to spend a lot to look nice. If you just focus on looking and feeling your best you will get what you desire both personally and professionally.

2

THOUGHTS/IMAGINATION

Imagine if everything that you thought about happened immediately. How would that affect your life? Was your first thought something negative or positive? In this chapter we will focus on what we take for granted, and our daily thoughts. What you think about a person, place, or thing effects what kind of roll that person, place or thing will play in your life. Most of you have heard the saying you are what you eat. In this chapter I will show you that you are what you think. There will be a few exercises later that will help you shape your thoughts. My goal is to show you ways to bring your wants and desires to you. All successful people have one thing in common. Before they reached any level of success they took the time to think about what they wanted. They used their imaginations to organize an attack plan and executed it. This process is used to perfection every day. It doesn't matter how big or small the goal. Let's talk about how to apply this process to your job search, promotion, or entrepreneurial quest. Let's do a brief exercise.

THOUGHTS/IMAGINATION

- Close your eyes and think of something or someone that makes you happy.

    Notice how your body feels. Are you relaxed? Do you feel like your mind is open to thoughts and feelings?

- Now close your eyes and think of something or someone that makes you angry.

    Notice your facial expressions. Are they tense? How about your hands are they clinched? When your mind is consumed with anger it is more likely that you become close minded.

That exercise was meant to make you aware of the power your mind possesses. Your mind is the cable box and your thoughts are the remote control. Your body then displays what you are thinking like a TV monitor would. This means that you control what characters people are watching when they see you. Think about it this way, life will always put things in your way to force you to make a discussion. Life will disturb you at the most unpredictable moments. How you react to those moments is what will either lead to an open door or a closed door. If you can take your thoughts and use your imagination to act those thoughts out in your mind you will achieve them. Here are two scenarios where thoughts and imagination either made the person or broke the person.

TURN YOUR COMMON SENSE INTO BUSINESS SAVVY

Scenario A

Maria has an interview for a job she has dreamed about. She has waited two years to get this interview, and she is on cloud 9. The night before the interview she hangs out with her friends for a celebration drink. When she gets home she eats a quick snack and watches TV. She falls asleep on the couch and wakes up the next morning 20 minutes later than she wanted. She had to pick out her clothes, iron them which took 30 minutes. That left her 20 minutes to shower, get dressed and make it to the interview early. She rushed out of the house leaving her resume on the kitchen counter. Traffic caused Maria to arrive only 2 minutes ahead of her schedule appointment time. She enters the office and is immediately escorted to the meeting room. When the interviewer enters the room he asked Maria for a resume. Maria explains that she was rushing and left it on the counter. Immediately she realizes that she lost creditability. Maria wonders what will happen next in the interview process. The interviewer informs Maria that he will ask a series of questions that pertain to the job. She is not prepared mentally for any of the questions which made her extremely nervous. Her body language showed her nervousness. To make things worst she was not confident in her answers. Maria's years of high level experience in the field was non-existent in the interview. She later found out via email that she was passed over for the position. Instead of trying again, Maria began to think negatively about

THOUGHTS/IMAGINATION

her abilities. Her fear of failing consumed her thoughts and she never applied for a higher position again.

Scenario B

Jennifer is scheduled for the same interview the next day. The night before the interview she picks out her suit, and irons it. She then places a copy of her resume in her car on the front seat so there would be no way to forget it. Instead of watching her favorite show she decides to do some research on the company. She finds some valuable information online and a series of good questions to ask during the interview. She then imagined that she was celebrating after she got the job and how good it would feel. Before lying down she had an amazing thought. Jennifer realized that being 30 minutes early would allow her to see the inner workings of the office. The next day Jennifer woke up on time. She got dressed and left the house 1 hour before her appointment time. She arrived at the interview site 35 minutes ahead of schedule. When she arrived the interviewer had not arrived yet. She took this opportunity to do what she imagined. After starting a conversation with the secretary she was able to find out more about the company's history and the day to day operations that goes on in the department she would potentially be working for. This new information gave Jennifer a huge edge and confidence boost. Jennifer's body language was amazingly positive and she presented herself as being extremely knowledgeable. She was

TURN YOUR COMMON SENSE
INTO BUSINESS SAVVY

hired on the spot and received $10,000 more in annual salary than she expected.

Looking at both scenarios what was the difference? Was one person more knowledgeable when it came to work experience? NO, the difference was Jennifer was prepared and had a mental game plan. She used the power of thought and imagination. You too have the power that Jennifer displayed. We are all born with it, some use it and others let it go to waste. If you can control your thoughts and what you daydream about every day you too can control your future. It's that simple! Here is what I did to get myself started on the road to success.

Every day I woke up and said out loud "Today I control my thoughts" I repeated that statement 5 times. Sometimes I would do it during the day just to get the mental energy I needed. That's the easy part; the hard part is what you do when a negative thought enters your mind. Thoughts like "don't go in there you are not dressed good enough", or "they don't like my kind of people in there". Here's is what you do; you say "They are going to love me". Positive mental power can overcome all.

In the last chapter we touched on image and the importance of first impression or perception. Now let's tie together chapter one and two. When you look good, and feel good people will notice you when you enter a room. Once they notice you they want to know who you are as a person. They do this so they can categorize

THOUGHTS/IMAGINATION

you for their own mental well-being. If they can identify you with someone they encountered in the past they will then know how to communicate with you. It is important that when they make that initial contact with you that your thoughts are positive. If you have imagined that whoever comes in contact with you will like you it will be so. If you do this, the energy that they will feel from you will be good. At the end of the day we are all energy beings. The energy you put out there is what you get back. Have you liked someone you just met and didn't know why? The reason you liked that person is because they had great energy. When you come into contact with positive energy it makes you feel good. You can also have the same effect on your life and people you meet in a negative manner. The choice is yours! This statement best sums up this chapter. "We are today what our thoughts were yesterday, and we will be tomorrow what our thoughts are today!"

3
COMMUNICATION

What is the definition of communication? Communication is the exchange of thoughts, messages, or information, as by speech, signals, writing, or behavior. The key word in this definition is "exchange"; in order to effectively communicate you must give and receive information. So many times we like to talk but have a hard time listening. Listening is the most important part of the communication process. You must not only listen with your ears, but you must listen with your eyes, mind, and heart. What do I mean by listen with your eyes, mind, and heart? It has been said that 8% of what people receive is actual words. The tone of voice that is being used is 39% of what you receive. Which leaves 55% to body language which is facial expressions, posture, and hand gestures? In order to be a great communicator you must first be a great observer. Watch facial expressions, posture, and hand gestures to determine how to effectively communicate with each individual. For example, if you notice that the person you are talking to does not use their hands

COMMUNICATION

when they speak. It would be fair to say there could be a chance that this person may be offended by someone who does. These little things can make or break you in interviews, business meetings, or daily conversations. I have done over 2,000 interviews in my career. If a person is soft spoken and shy my first thought is they lack confidence. If a person is loud and giving forced eye contact my first thought is this person is over confident borderline cocky. These thoughts all come from voice tone and body language. The only time I focus on actual words when interviewing is if I ask a specific question that only requires one answer. I can't stress enough the importance of body language and tone. Here are 5 tips that may help you send off the right message when in a business meeting/interview.

- Step one: When you first establish contact with the person you are meeting, you must make eye contact and smile. This lets the person know you have a level of respect for them and have anticipated the meeting.

- Step two: You must let the person know you have awareness. You can do this by commenting positively on their attire or the overall environment.

- Step three: Think before you speak. Take your time and don't try to use big words. Pick words that can be understood by any age group. Because you are 100% certain of the meaning

TURN YOUR COMMON SENSE INTO BUSINESS SAVVY

it allows you to speak the words with confidence. This will guarantee your thoughts will be comprehended accurately. The worst fear of most people is public speaking. It is because no one wants to trip on words or sound less intelligent. If you stick to simple words it's a win for both parties.

- Step four: You must use the same body language as your interviewer. If they are speaking with their hands you do the same. If they are using facial expression as they speak you do the same. If they are doing neither of the two, then you do the same. This will make sure the focus is on the process and not your physical movements.

- Step five: You must not interrupt when the other person is speaking. While they are speaking you should be making eye contact, and acknowledging what is said with a simple head nod every 45 seconds. Why every 45 seconds? It is believed when a person is just continuously nodding their head they are not paying attention. When it is your turn to speak if needed you can look away for no more than 5 seconds. Then re-establish the eye contact and speak loud and clear.

We have gone over how to effectively communicate in a business meeting or interview. In this segment

COMMUNICATION

I would like to address the importance of the K.I.S.S method. There are several different versions, for me this stands for Keep It Short and Sharp. How many times have you listened to a speaker and all of a sudden your mind drifts elsewhere? It happens to the best listeners, I think most people just have trouble listening for long periods of time. How long do you think the average mind can focus before drifting? I am no scientist so I don't claim to have the answer to that question. What I can tell you is that after 25 seconds I am beginning to change focus. It generally takes me 30 seconds to return my focus. By that time how much information did I lose? The only way I can pick back up on the conversation is by using context clues. This is not that effective in the grand scheme of things. So in important situations I force myself to take notes, this keeps me engaged and informed. Feel free to use that technique it works. We can agree that being an active listener can be hard at times. How do you keep people focused on what you are trying to say? There is only one way to do that, by using the K.I.S.S method. It will keep your verbal message under 30 seconds. If you can be short, informative, graphic, and energetic you will keep everyone's attention. Which will make your message that more powerful. This method will also gain the respect of the people who you interact with. They will perceive you to be efficient and knowledgeable. How do you get your message out in less than 30 seconds? The answer to that question is practice. In chapter two we talked

TURN YOUR COMMON SENSE
INTO BUSINESS SAVVY

about thoughts and imagination. That will come into play when practicing your message. Here is the order in which you must organize your thoughts and message.

1. Identify your message
2. Determine what you want to achieve from this message
3. Imagine who may be receiving your message
4. What will get their attention (a joke, picture, serious matter, etc.)
5. Put your message together with what will get their attention.
6. Deliver your message in the correct vocal tone.
7. Last thing to do is imagine they will understand your message and that there will be smiling faces looking back at you.

If you follow these 7 steps you will find yourself able to express your feelings on the highest level. Here is an example. When I was 25 I interviewed for a General Manager position with a well-known restaurant group. During the interview I was asked a question that if answered correctly I knew I would land the position. The question was "Describe your leadership style and how you would get the staff to follow your lead as a General Manager?" Before I answered the question I realized that tone, body language, and eye contact was the key here. My answer had to show my previous experience with such a task. My goal was to achieve confidence

COMMUNICATION

from my interviewer by showing I had the ability to excel under pressure. I knew what type of GM the interviewer was looking to hire so I used my imagination to pick the correct words that would get his attention. I knew that my tone could not be too low or too high it had to be stern but softened with a consistent smile as I spoke. I then thought once I was finished he would nod in agreement. As you can see I went through each step and formulated my plan of action. Here is what I said verbatim.

"That's a great question. I believe my style is very demanding but fair. I will never ask my employees to do anything that I would not do. I believe every staff member has to be managed differently under the umbrella of the overall rules. In order to properly accomplish that you must be a listen first leader. In order to get any human being to believe in you there must be a level of respect. I think that leading from within is the only way to get that respect. This means that I will lead by example first. In an out of the business environment because whether you know it or not you are now a role model. Having a positive impact on a person's life is something I take very seriously. I welcome the challenge you will be setting before me. Being able to lead a team is the most important aspect of being a GM in my opinion."

This message was under 30 seconds and to the point. I was offered the position on the spot. We have gone over Image, Thoughts and Imagination, and now

TURN YOUR COMMON SENSE INTO BUSINESS SAVVY

Communication. Please take the time to review each section if needed. Communication is the best skill you can develop. It will not only land that job you want, but it will make you a better husband/wife, parent, friend and person. They say closed mouths don't get fed. Well closed ears don't get you ahead. Listening is just as important as speaking in the communication process. It is the combination of the two that will move you forward. Keep in mind before you can communicate you must first think.

4

ATTITUDE/ENERGY

When most people think of the word attitude a negative thought comes to mind. Growing up when I heard the word it was used in a negative manner. Mostly used to describe my body language towards something I didn't like. This made me think that my attitude was a product of my environment. I believed that because I grew up in a certain neighborhood that I adapted the attitude and energy of that community. There were times when I was younger that I wished I grew up in the suburbs or in a different state. I didn't know better, knowledge is power. I now know that attitude starts within you. How you respond to any situation will determine whether your attitude is positive or negative.

Why is attitude important in the business world? No employer wants to have someone on staff that is hard to communicate with. It makes the environment uncomfortable and unproductive. If people think that you are not approachable, your days with the company are numbered. If the person you are interviewing with for a job sees potential for a bad attitude you will not

TURN YOUR COMMON SENSE INTO BUSINESS SAVVY

be hired. I played football from the age of 9 until I was 25. The number one thing that every coach preached was attitude and energy. In the work environment companies want a team player; someone who understands that there will be adversity, but no matter what you will stay on the course and remain positive. That you will not only keep a good attitude but that your attitude will lift the energy of the people around you. In the restaurant field it is so important to have a good attitude and energy. When I interview potential team members this is what I look for first. I can teach them how to make drinks, take care of guests, and use the computer systems. What I can't teach is attitude and energy either they have it or they don't.

There are three types of potential employees. There is yes, maybe, or no it is that simple. The question is how do you get from being a no to yes? The answer to that question is having positive energy and a great attitude. Stereotypes play into how people perceive your attitude or energy. Here are 10 things that will make people think you have a bad attitude or energy.

1. Visible tattoos in certain areas
2. Not wearing the right clothes
3. If you use slang words
4. Not Saying please and thank you (appreciate it doesn't count as a thank you)
5. Bad walking habits and bad posture while sitting

ATTITUDE/ENERGY

6. If you don't make eye contact
7. Bad hygiene/length and cleanliness of nails
8. The tone in which you speak
9. Not smiling
10. Not asking the key questions

Now let's go through each stereotype and deliver an attack plan.

- Visible tattoos, this is a huge issue for most employers. Wear clothing that will cover any tattoos whether you feel they are offensive or not. This allows the focus to be on you and your experience. Once you have completed the interview process you should ask about their tattoo policy.

- Not wearing the right clothes, what does this mean? When going to an interview simple is always better. Stay away from short shirts, tight pants; see through shirts, and bright colors. Gray, blue, dark green, white (shirt only), and black are the colors that I recommend. Your shirt should be tucked in nice and neat. Wearing a belt is a must.

- Do not use slang words when talking to anyone during a business meeting or interview. If the person interviewing you tries to lure you in don't take the bait. It is a set up; they want to see if what you are showing them is an act. Use

TURN YOUR COMMON SENSE INTO BUSINESS SAVVY

the tips from Chapter 3 to help you with this.

- Saying Please and Thank You is a direct reflection of your mental growth. Most people view that as direct reflection on how you were raised by your parents. If they feel that you had no parental guidance they will view you as troubled or negative person. Although this is unfortunate, it is the absolute truth. You must keep your personal life completely separate from the work environment.

- Bad walking habits and posture; you must have a smooth steady walk when approaching your interviewer. Any hitch in your get up is not a good thing. If you have an injury of course there is nothing you can do about that. Posture while sitting says a lot about your discipline. You should be sitting upright and attentive.

- Eye contact we went over in Chapter 3 again very important. It is both respectful and informative about you as a person.

- Hygiene, ladies long nails although pretty they are not business appropriate. Bright colors take the focus away from what you are saying and put them on your nails. Men shaving is a must, being clean cut says that you pay attention to detail.

- The tone of your voice is very important in any environment. In chapter 3 we went over the

ATTITUDE/ENERGY

importance of tone in your voice, again it is 39% percent of the message received.

- Smiling, if your eyes are the window to your soul, your smile is the window to your personality. Smile and smile often.
- Asking the right questions in an interview shows that you did your research. It is vital to ask questions after the initial employment history segment is completed.

If you follow these guidelines you will put yourself in a position to get the job every time. From that point on it will be about experience and knowledge.

Attitude and Energy starts when you wake up in the morning. You have to be strong mentally; you cannot let anyone or anything control your mood. No one said it would be easy right away. Life rewards the ones who put in the work to be great. Doesn't matter the challenge if you can see yourself overcoming, it will be so. The work starts with believing and imagining that you can do it. The rest will work itself out if you stay positive with your attitude and energy. You control your destiny not the environment where you were raised. The only person to blame if you don't become who want is you.

5

LOVE

What do you want out of life? Do you want cars, a companion, money, a house, or a loving family? All the things that we may want in life come with one key component. That component is love; love is what drives us to want various things in life. There is not a day that goes by that I don't imagine my life either loving or being loved by something or someone. I once asked a successful business woman who was at the top in her career field. How does it feel to be the best in your field? Her response was "it would be great if I had someone to share my success with".

We all want to be loved or have love for a material object or person. This love is what you need to tap into every day. There is an element of success that is overlooked consistently. That element is emotion. Emotion is the most powerful thing we possess as human beings. You can do things beyond your imagination if you are emotionally invested in the task at hand. So many times we get caught up on making money that we lose sight of the goal. The goal is to obtain whatever it is you love, and be loved while doing it. Here is a Greek mythology story about love that has always intrigued me.

Pyramus and Thisbe. Their story described a selfless love and they made sure that even in death, they were together. Pyramus was a very handsome man and was the childhood friend of Thisbe, the fairest maiden in Babylonia. They both lived in neighboring homes and fell in love with each other as they grew up together. However, their parents were dead against them marrying each other. So one night just before the crack of dawn, while everyone was asleep, they decided to slip out of their homes and meet in the nearby fields near a mulberry tree. Thisbe reached there first. As she waited under the tree, she saw a lion coming near the spring close by to quench its thirst. Its jaws were bloody. When Thisbe saw this horrifying sight, she panicked and ran to hide behind some hollow rocks nearby. As she was running, she dropped her veil. The lion came near and picked up the veil in his bloody jaws. At that moment, Pyramus reaches near the mulberry tree and sees Thisbe's veil in the jaws of the lion. He is completely devastated. Shattered, he pierces his chest with his own sword. Unknown to what just happened; Thisbe is still hiding in the rocks due to the fear of the lion. When she comes out after sometime, she sees what her lover did to himself. She is totally shattered when she sees the sword piercing right through her lover's chest. She also takes the sword and kills herself. This is an extreme version of what effect love and emotion can have on

TURN YOUR COMMON SENSE INTO BUSINESS SAVVY

people; her devotion to him was unmatched.

How does this tie into the overall goal of becoming business savvy? If you don't love your job it is a matter of time before you leave. The number one reason people leave a job is feeling unappreciated. Or for the purpose of this chapter not feeling loved. Your work is a product of you, a birth of your thoughts, time, and physical labor. If you are emotionally invested in your work and the company it will show. The only way to become invested in a potential company is to learn about their history. Understand why it was started, and who benefits when they do well. Finding that love or emotional drive for your job sounds easier said than done. So how can you find love doing something that you know is not your dream? Before you love something you must first understand it. Think about a food item that you may or may not like. Most people have a list of things that cause them to dislike or like that food item. Depending on these feelings you either eat that food or stay clear of it. Finding a job is not just about the money, it must be about the feeling. The basic principles of that job must be in line with the things you love. Let's take a step back and start at the basic level of where love is produced.

Love can be both productive and destructive, please allow me to explain. In order to love any place, person, or thing we must first love ourselves. At the core of productive love is caring of self. You must be able to sustain your mental happiness on your own. Once you are

LOVE

able to do this than you can share that love or positive energy. If you do not have love for yourself problems can occur. What happens is you become dependent on the high of someone else's positive energy or love. This can be addictive like drugs or alcohol. If you only take a person's positive energy without giving positive energy they will become drained and detach themselves from you. There must be an even exchange of positive energy or love to make it blissful for both people.

The same love principles apply to the business world. Each person in your company is putting a piece of themselves into their work. Just like a proud parent they are emotionally attached to what they produce. If one person is not taking the job seriously it creates tension. The people that are emotionally invested in their work take offense to that person's lack of devotion. This is why it is important to find work that relates to who you are. If you are invested in the job emotionally you will produce better work. If you produce better work the other staff members who are invested emotionally like you will notice. When they notice your level of commitment you become beloved. When you become beloved you and your work are now essential. When you become essential to the company you get more money. That is how the cycle of business works. This book is not just about you working for someone. It is about you reaching whatever dreams you have. These principles can be applied to interviewing, job promotions, or entrepreneurial ventures.

TURN YOUR COMMON SENSE INTO BUSINESS SAVVY

Let's look at the story of James. James was raised in a household where love and drugs went hand in hand. His parents taught him manners, to fear God, and love your family. They also showed him a life of partying, drinking and drugs. Growing up in this household James never wanted for anything. All the new toys, bikes, or clothes he wanted he got them. All good things not obtained by good must come to an end. James found himself and his family homeless. He then resorted to what he grew up watching, the life of drinking and drugs. James had a dream though; his dream was to be a respected businessman. He knew that in order to do that he would have to excel at something. Growing up he was one of the top football players in the area. He turned his focus to sports, but never lost focus of being a successful businessman. After years of hard labor and struggle, James found himself playing college football. He tried to make it to the NFL but was not fast enough. He then turned to the dream he had of being a successful businessman. He imagined himself in a suit and tie running a successful company. He would see nice cars and imagine himself driving them. After college he decided to relocate to a different state with no job, car or place to live. He had a friend that let him sleep on his living room floor for a few months. During this time, James formed a plan in his mind. The plan was to stay positive and to think as if he had already reached his dream. He started by dressing in his one suit every day to feel as if he already made

LOVE

his goal. The next step was every morning he would imagine a business card with his name on it and the title General Manager. He landed his first job in the area within 2 days of starting this new plan. He was hired as a Kitchen Manager but two weeks later the General Manager was fired. They offered him the job and James was now the General Manager of the establishment. This was only three weeks after he started this new plan.

James was happy but he knew this was not his ultimate goal. He took the money he made to get more clothing and a vehicle. Now he was able to drive into different areas to find better opportunities. He worked on his communication skills by studying body language and how people received different gestures. He began preparing for future interviews with bigger companies he kept notes on and all the systems he created. A few years later he interviewed for a better position and got the job. Unfortunately, he was not received well by his co-workers at the beginning. James remained positive and people took notice of it. 18 months later James was in charge of the biggest store in the company. He eventually made a name for himself around the city. Over time his dream took him on a search for a better opportunity. By this time owners took notice of his skill set and offered James a better position. He never lost sight of who he wanted to be through all the hard work and success. 5 years passed and James noticed that he was losing what made him great. He was becoming a

TURN YOUR COMMON SENSE
INTO BUSINESS SAVVY

clock puncher and lost the love for his work. He knew that starting his own company was the only thing that would keep him invested emotionally. He used his image, thoughts, imagination, communication, love, and formed a new plan. After rediscovering his passion James finally decided to start his own consulting company; finally reaching his goal of ownership.

This is how you put the 5 principles of this book to work. I know this story very well because the story of James is really my story. I must say that the road will always have challenges. Stay positive don't let anyone or anything stop you from being great. This book is not just about finding a job, interviewing well, or becoming an owner of a business. It is about finding yourself. I hope you see that the answer you have been searching for is inside of you. Take the time to think, pray, imagine and the life you seek will be yours.